W9-DFU-060

The Thingumajig Book of Manners

Story by
Irene Keller

Illustrations by
Dick Keller

Ideals Publishing Corp.
Milwaukee, Wisconsin

ISBN 0-8249-8010-7

Thingumajigs
Eat toads and snails
And pick their teeth
With their fingernails.

I brush
after
meals!

They slurp their soup,
They rock their chairs,
And they eat their dinner
In their underwear.

My table manners are the best you'll ever see. It's always such a pleasure when you eat with me.

They never use napkins,
They dribble and drool,
And they always talk
When their mouths are full.

I
eat
neatly!

They eat like pigs,
Those Thingumajigs!

I get all my vitamins and eat the way I
should. Just a little of what you fancy does
you such a lot of good.

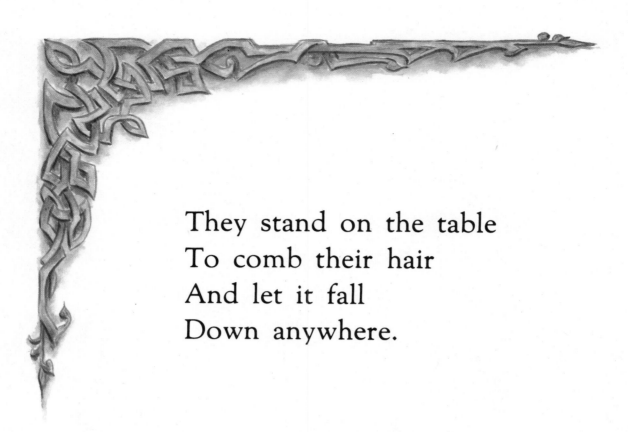

They stand on the table
To comb their hair
And let it fall
Down anywhere.

That's a
definite
no-no!

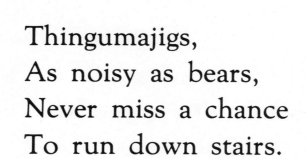

Thingumajigs,
As noisy as bears,
Never miss a chance
To run down stairs.

It's fun to run, but *not*
indoors and *never* on stairs
or polished floors.

They never say "Thank you,"
And they never say "Please,"
And they never use a tissue
When they cough or sneeze.

Minding our manners means thinking of others—our friends and our teachers, our sisters and brothers, our grandmas and grandpas, our fathers and mothers.

Rude words, bad words,
Mumbles and grunts,
Those Thingumajigs
All talk at once.

Waiting our turn and
"Excuse me, please," help
us out of spots like these.

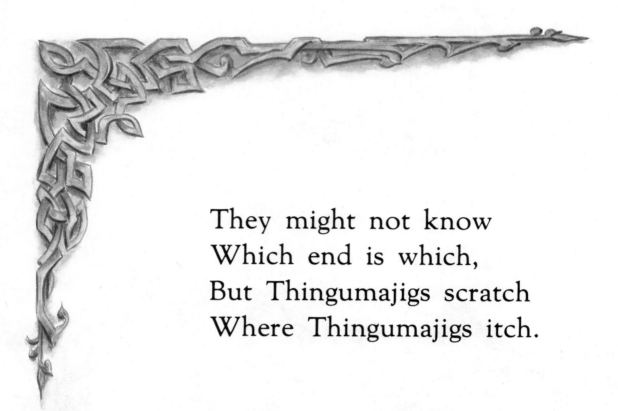

They might not know
Which end is which,
But Thingumajigs scratch
Where Thingumajigs itch.

That's gross!

Wash away
your wildlife!

They kick, they bite,
They scream, they fight,
But they never say "Good Morning,"
And they never say "Good Night."

Good words and cheerful smiles, I've found, help to make the world go round.

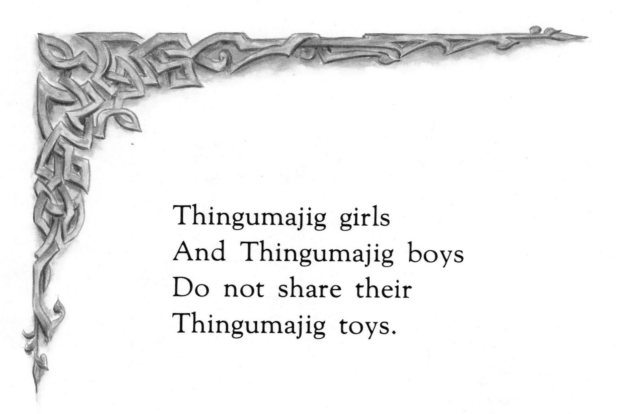

Thingumajig girls
And Thingumajig boys
Do not share their
Thingumajig toys.

Learning to share is learning to grow. That's what life's about, you know.

Thingumajigs sulk
And Thingumajigs say,
"If I won't win
Then I won't play."

Good sports do the best they can.
We can do the same.
We win some and we lose some,
but we're always in the game.

They don't clean up
And they don't do chores,
But they're very good
At slamming doors.

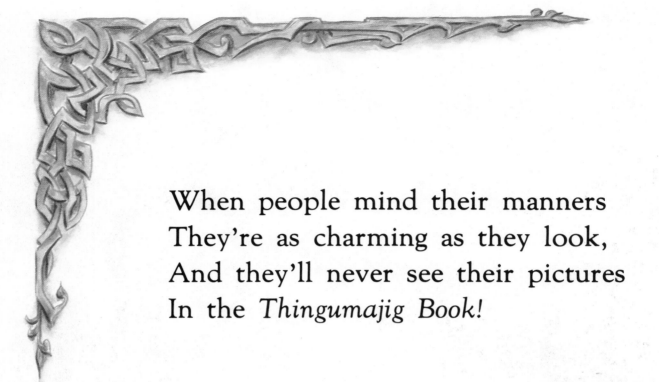

When people mind their manners
They're as charming as they look,
And they'll never see their pictures
In the *Thingumajig Book!*